a gift for

from

## OTHER GIFTBOOKS BY HELEN EXLEY:

To a very special Daughter     A gem of a Daughter

To a very special Son     To a very special Mother

You're a great Son

## OTHER BOOKS IN THIS SERIES:

Poor Mum!     A Woman's Work is Never Done

Girl Talk!     Too Soon for a Mid-Life Crisis

But it's My Turn to Sulk!

Published in 2010 by Helen Exley Giftbooks in Great Britain

12  11  10  9  8  7  6  5  4  3  2  1

Design, selection and arrangement copyright © 2010 Helen Exley
Cartoons copyright © 2010 Rowan Barnes-Murphy
The moral right of the authors has been asserted.

ISBN: 978-1-84634-452-7

Acknowledgements: The publishers are grateful for permission to reproduce copyright
material. Whilst every effort has been made to trace copyright holders, we would be
pleased to hear from any not here acknowledged. BILL COSBY: from FATHERHOOD by
Bill Cosby, published by G P Putnam's Sons, an imprint of Penguin Group (USA) Inc.
GARRISON KEILLOR: from A PRAIRIE HOME COMPANION WITH GARRISON
KEILLOR radio show. FRED SCHOENBERG: from MIDDLE AGE RAGE AND OTHER
INDIGNITIES by Fred Schoenberg, published by Simon and Schuster.
IMPORTANT COPYRIGHT NOTICE: PAM BROWN, PAMELA DUGDALE,
CHARLOTTE GRAY, PETER GRAY, STUART AND LINDA MACFARLANE AND
SIÀN E. MORGAN are all © Helen Exley 2010.

*To the memory of Hugh – a great Dad and a great Grandad.*

**Helen Exley Giftbooks, 16 Chalk Hill, Watford, Herts, WD19 4BG, UK**
**www.helenexleygiftbooks.com**

# POOR DAD!

## A SPECIAL THANK YOU

ROWAN BARNES-MURPHY

A father is for being
talked into being a butterfly
in my school play.

ROBIN ROSENBALM, AGE 11

However much
he steels himself
no dad is prepared for
the telephone bill.

PAM BROWN, B.1928

Fathers know their place —
last in the line
for the shower and
first in the line to pay for everything.

STUART & LINDA MACFARLANE

If a man smiles at home somebody
is sure to ask him for money.

WILLIAM FEATHER (1908-1976)

A dad is a sports car driver who has temporarily forsaken his passion for sports cars to drive a family saloon.

STUART & LINDA MACFARLANE

There are two classes of travel — first class and with children.

ROBERT BENCHLEY (1889-1945)

And that's the wonderful thing about family travel: it provides you with experiences that will remain locked forever in the scar tissue of your mind.

DAVE BARRY

One day, you're cruising down life's fast lane with the top down, wind in your hair and "Born to Be Wild" blaring on the stereo. The next thing you know, you're singing silly songs about some old man who plays knickknack paddywhack...

JIM PARKER

Dads at the wheel must learn that when The Youngest Child insists he needs to poo, wee or be sick *now*, he means it.

PAM BROWN, B.1928

When toy guides say
"from three years upwards",
the "upwards" bit
is referring to your dad.

SIÀN E. MORGAN, B.1973

A child is the perfect excuse to have
your second childhood. Now you can buy
all the trains, dolls and teddies
you've been wanting for so long.

STUART & LINDA MACFARLANE

In every real man a child is hidden
who wants to play.

FRIEDRICH NIETZSCHE (1844-1900)

The child had every toy their
father wanted.

ROBERT C. WHITTEN

# A CHILD HIRES
# AND ENSLAVES YOU.

## PROVERB

If you want to have power
go into politics. If you want to be
a decision-maker become a consultant.
But if you'd rather work like a slave,
be constantly insulted and
frequently ignored,
then "father" is the job for you.

STUART & LINDA MACFARLANE

# THE LAST STRAW!

The one thing
children wear out
faster than shoes
is parents.

JOHN J. PLOMP

Dads are
helpful round
the house.
But they draw the line
at cat sick.

PAM BROWN, B.1928

A dad discovers
soon after
his baby is born that
Things Will
Never Be
The Same Again.

PETER DE VRIES

Adieu long lie-ins on weekends.
Adieu grabbing a small bag
and a passport, and disappearing to
Patagonia for a month.
Adieu traveling lightly through life.
Children demand your complete
attention. They become
your foremost personal and fiscal
priority. They take over your life —
and, of course, you wouldn't
want it any other way.

DOUGLAS KENNEDY

A dad looking down on his newborn baby
would give it anything, everything.
He little knows that is exactly what will
be expected.

PAM BROWN, B.1928

Baby may seem sweet and
innocent but she has
an important duty to perform.
She has the difficult job of
"father-trainer". Inevitably, within
days of the birth, Dad
will be scurrying around, diapers
and soothers in hand,
obeying baby's every wailing
demand for attention.

STUART & LINDA MACFARLANE

A baby's thumb is minuscule –
but its father is firmly under it.

PAM BROWN, B.1928

Dad has long and earnest
conversations with his baby daughter.
He tells her
she is noisy, undisciplined and
manipulative – and she will
be sent back if she doesn't
pull herself together.
And the baby smiles complacently.
She has him exactly
where she wants him.

PAM BROWN. B.1928


HOW DO YOU SPOT A NEW FATHER?
He has not slept for 72 hours
and yawns constantly.
He has sick running down his jacket collar.
He is smiling moronically with sheer
delight and happiness.

STUART & LINDA MACFARLANE

There must be a
training school somewhere
that teaches dads of all ages
how to blow raspberries,
make funny noises
and pull their ears out
as far as they can go.

SIÀN E. MORGAN, B.1973

Nothing I have ever done has given me more joys and rewards than being a father to my children.

BILL COSBY, B.1937

# Your Dad is There
# to add sparkle and surprise
# to your childhood.

SIAN E. MORGAN, B.1973

A successful dad is good.
A loving, gentle dad is better.

PETER GRAY

A dad's love wraps us round
and keeps us warm and safe
till the end of our days.

PAM BROWN, B.1928

# Everyone needs
a wonderful father
– and I've got one!

PAMELA DUGDALE

Here's my dear dad.
There's no one in
the whole world like him.
And I love every bit of him.

PETER GRAY

# DEAR DAD

You will not let me fall.
You will keep enemies at bay.
You will give me comfort
and laughter
and praise.

PAM BROWN, B.1928

When a child is very small
Dad can keep you from all harm….
Boggarts and Ghosties and
Things-that-live-under-the-bed.
Dad wishes he could work the same magic
all your life.
He will try his very best.

CHARLOTTE GRAY

# My Diamond Dad.
# The jewel
# in my Crown.

PAM BROWN, B.1928

A good dad holds the home
and family together.
They are inclined to shrink
with the passing years.
But are still a good ten foot tall
in their children's eyes.

CHARLOTTE GRAY

Dad's love becomes a part of us
that can never be lost.

PAMELA DUGDALE

A dad sees the artistic genius
in his child's first scribbles
and is able to find parallels with
the work of Picasso.

…

Being a father means watching your young
daughter perform her magic trick
for the hundredth time and still acting
amazed when the coin disappears.

STUART & LINDA MACFARLANE

# Dads are required to know absolutely everything.

PETER GRAY

Grown-ups never understand anything
for themselves, and it is tiresome
for children to be always and forever
explaining things to them.

ANTOINE DE SAINT-EXUPÉRY (1900-1944),
FROM "THE LITTLE PRINCE"

You have to love
your dad very much
when he comes last in
the Father's Race
for the third year running.

PAM BROWN, B.1928

OK. You're a successful executive.
You run a splendid car.
You speak four languages.
But you fell flat in the Sack Race
on Sports Day.

PETER GRAY

Dads told
to watch
the saucepan
eventually
just have
to send out
for a takeaway.

CHARLOTTE GRAY

Every dad
has his
kitchen
speciality.
My dad's
is Beans
on Toast.

PAMELA DUGDALE

A dad is a person that
thinks he knows everything
but he doesn't even
understand
simple new math.

MELISSA WELLINGTON, AGE 10

Over the years, helping with homework,
dads discover how very little they
learned at school.

PAM BROWN, B.1928

You know you're over forty when —
you can no longer help the kids
with their homework.
On the parts you help with, they get 'C-'.

HERBERT I. KAVET,
FROM "YOU KNOW YOU'RE OVER 40 WHEN..."

"Parents are strange,"
said Amy,
"for their age."

AMANDA VAIL

Dads should applaud you
in the school play.
But not jump up
and shout "Bravo!" and "Encore!"

PETER GRAY

Only a dad would cause you the double
embarrassment of video recording your
performance in the school play and
then insisting on showing it to everyone
who visits.

STUART MACFARLANE, B.1953

Parents are not
quite interested in justice,
they are interested in quiet.

BILL COSBY, B.1937,
FROM "FATHERHOOD"

No one can say
of his house,
"There is no Trouble here."

ORIENTAL PROVERB

Dads run with you
part of the way.
But get out of puff.
Are forced to stop
and wave you on.
Smiling to see you speed away.

CHARLOTTE GRAY

Dads grow old and creak a little
— but their hearts are young.

PAM BROWN, B.1928

# Dads~ dear, Daft, TOTALLY out of date dads.

PAM BROWN, B.1928

Only a dad would cause you the
embarrassment of stopping the school show,
in mid performance, while he replaces the
battery in his video camera.

STUART MACFARLANE, B.1953

Poor Dad.
It's hard to be a Hero
all the time.

PAM BROWN, B.1928

# POOR. DAD. DEAR DAD.
# HE MEANS WELL.

PAM BROWN, B.1928

There comes a sad moment
when your children
realize you don't know everything.

PETER GRAY

Remember, if your teenager doesn't think you
are a real embarrassment
and a hard-nosed bore,
you are probably not doing your job.

H. JACKSON BROWN, JR

W hat I have learned
in the process of raising [four]
daughters — and perhaps it applies
to other human affairs as well
— is that there is no single answer,
no magic formula,
no rigid set of guidelines,
no simple blueprint,
no book of easy instructions,
no sure way of
side-stepping difficulties,
no easy way out. There is love.

GEORGE LEONARD

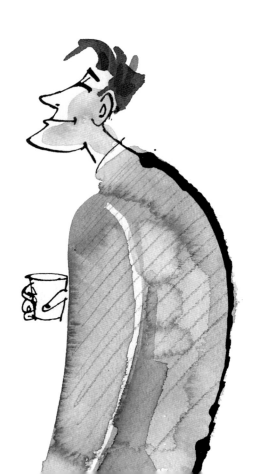

# Trials of a father...

No man knows his true character
until he has run out of gas,
purchased something on the installment plan
and raised an adolescent.

MARCELENE COX

When our phone rings, it's always
for my daughter. When it isn't ringing,
it's because she's talking on it.
Sometimes when she's on our phone,
the people next door will come over
and tell her she's wanted on their phone.

ART FRANK

One day Dad will get to the bathroom first.

PETER GRAY

# DADS THINK THEIR DAUGHTERS ARE PERFECT ~ BUT A BIT UNNERVING.

CHARLOTTE GRAY

The father of a daughter,
especially one in her teens, will
find that she doesn't like to be
seen walking with him on the street.
In fact, she will often ask him
to walk a few paces behind.
The father should not take
this outdoor demotion personally;
it is simply a matter
of clothes.
His are rotten.

BILL COSBY, B.1937
FROM "FATHERHOOD"

A father may not have all the answers
but he sure has all the problems.

STUART & LINDA MACFARLANE

...how does a father feel? Tired, certainly.
Harassed, probably. Scared, sometimes.
Satisfied, absolutely.
And yes, very, very grown up.

PETER HOWARTH, FROM "SECOND
CHILDHOOD" IN "FATHERHOOD"

Try to remember that,
with the exception of your parents
and your children, most people
will consider you an adult.

FRED SCHOENBERG, FROM
"MIDDLE AGE RAGE AND OTHER MALE INDIGNITIES"

As a father of two there is a respectful
question which I wish to ask of fathers of
five: How do you happen to be still alive?

OGDEN NASH (1902-1971)

# DADS MEAN TO BE FIRM WITH DAUGHTERS. BUT GIRLS CRY.

PAM BROWN, B.1928

The father of a daughter
is nothing but a high-class hostage,
but when his daughter puts her arm
over his shoulder and says,
"Daddy, I need to ask you something,"
he is a pat of butter in a hot frying pan.

GARRISON KEILLOR, B.1942

I told myself that
when my daughters were
twenty-one I'd stop worrying.
I didn't. Then I said
when they got married
I'd stop worrying.
I didn't.
Now all this worrying
is starting to worry me.

LEE IACOCCA, B.1924

When I was a boy of fourteen,
my father was so ignorant
I could hardly stand to have
the old man around.
But when I got to be
twenty-one, I was astonished
at how much he
had learned in seven years.

MARK TWAIN (1835-1910)


Before I got married I had six theories
about bringing up children.
Now I have six children and no theories.

JOHN WILMOT (1647-1680)
[LORD ROCHESTER]

Dear Dad. I love you
— every white hair.
Every wrinkle.
I think I gave you most of them.
Wear them with pride.

PAM BROWN, B.1928

My dear Dad.
Here are all the sorries that I owe you.
Tied up with love.

CHARLOTTE GRAY

# Dearest Dad.
Everyone knows
your jokes by heart.
That's why they are so special.

PAM BROWN, B.1928

There is no one quite like you, Dad.
A one-off.
A Limited Edition.
The dearest, funniest, kindest dad of all.

CHARLOTTE GRAY

# HELEN EXLEY

Helen Exley is well-known for her
collections of quotations, with her giftbooks
selling five million copies a year
in thirty five languages.
Her books are on family, friends and love,
with a strong inspirational addition of
wisdom, personal peace and values books.

*Poor Dad!* is the sequel to *Poor Mum! Poor Mum!* has
been doing amazingly well, with everyone worrying
about how hard-done-by mothers have so much to
bear... But then the protests started! I had ignored
Dads; "Dads also need a special thank-you." "No one
notices that fathers often have to do everything a
mother does these days – sometimes more..."
And, "Dads love is utterly central in a happy family."
So here is the sequel by popular protest –
crammed with patronising, adoring, happy, rude
and absolutely hilarious tributes to the poor guy.
The message is clear... never, ever
ignore a good dad, whose love and strength
and care is with you for life.

# Rowan Barnes-Murphy

Rowan Barnes-Murphy's cartoons are wicked, spiky and frayed at the edges. His fantastically well-observed characters are hugely popular and have been used to advertise a diverse range of products such as cars, clothes and phones, supermarkets, bank accounts and greeting cards.

**Other books in this series:**
Too Soon for a Mid-Life Crisis
A Woman's Work is Never Done
Poor Mum!
But it's My Turn to Sulk!

For more information contact:
**Helen Exley Giftbooks, 16 Chalk Hill, Watford, Herts, WD19 4BG, UK.**

Helen Exley giftbooks are all on our website. Have a look… maybe you will find many more intriguing gift ideas!

**www.helenexleygiftbooks.com**